Nature's Glory

an uplifting coloring book
by Christina Rose

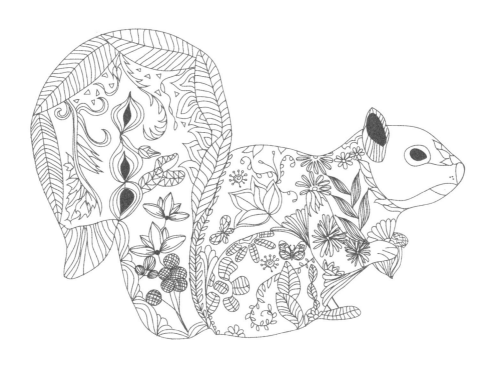

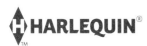

Nature's Glory
an uplifting coloring book

ISBN-13: 978-0-373-09998-6'

First published in the United States and Canada in 2016 by
Harlequin Books S.A.

Copyright © Bell & Mackenzie Publishing Limited 2015
This edition published by arrangement with Bell & Mackenzie Publishing Ltd.
and Harlequin Books S.A.

Created by Christina Rose
Contributors: Letitia Clouden

www.bellmackenzie.com

www.Harlequin.com

Printed in U.S.A.

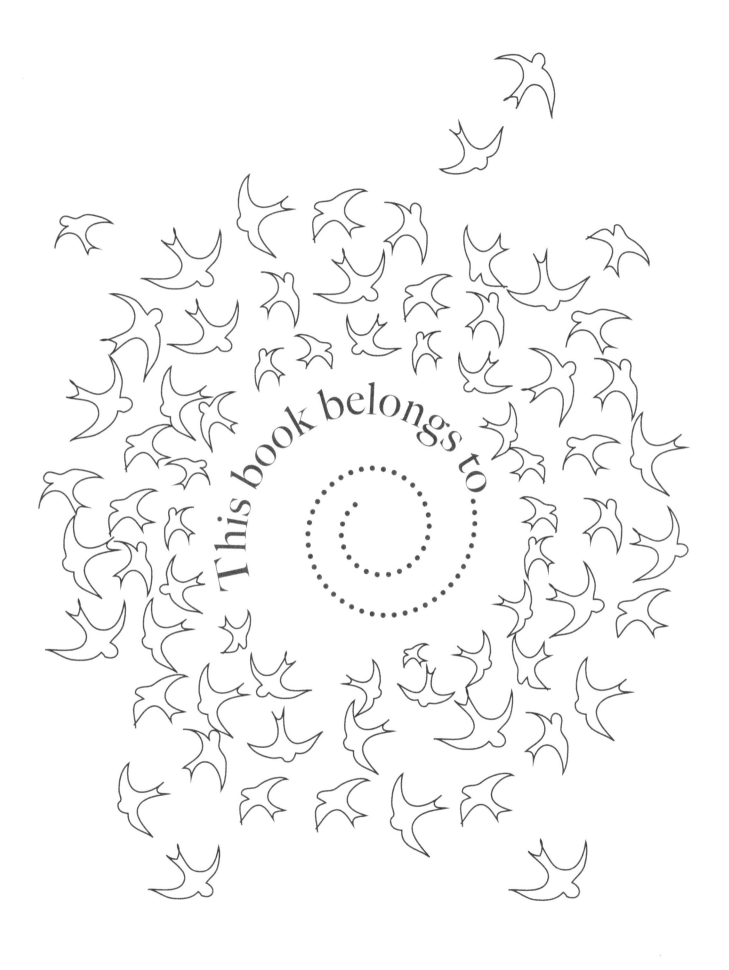

This book belongs to ....

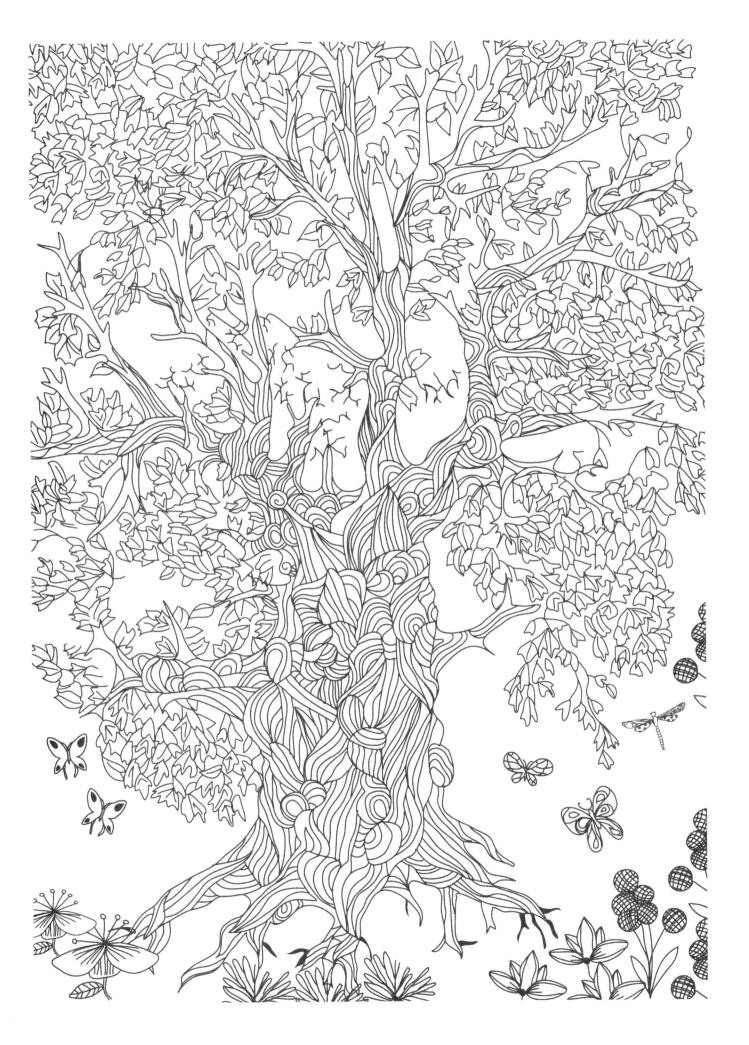

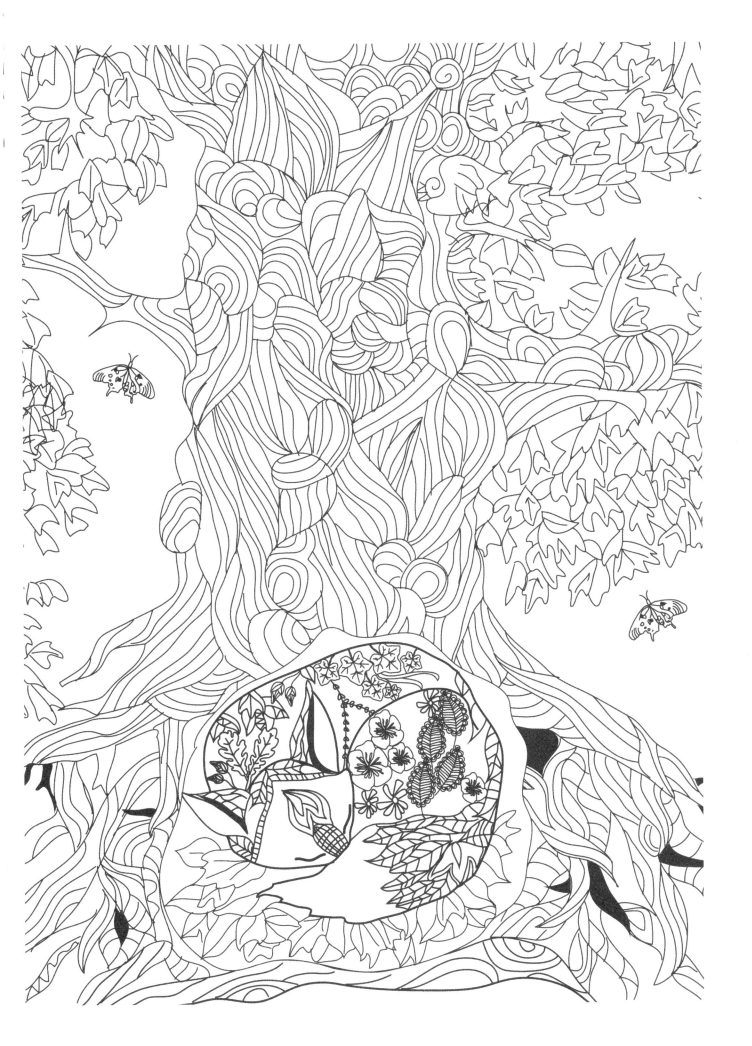

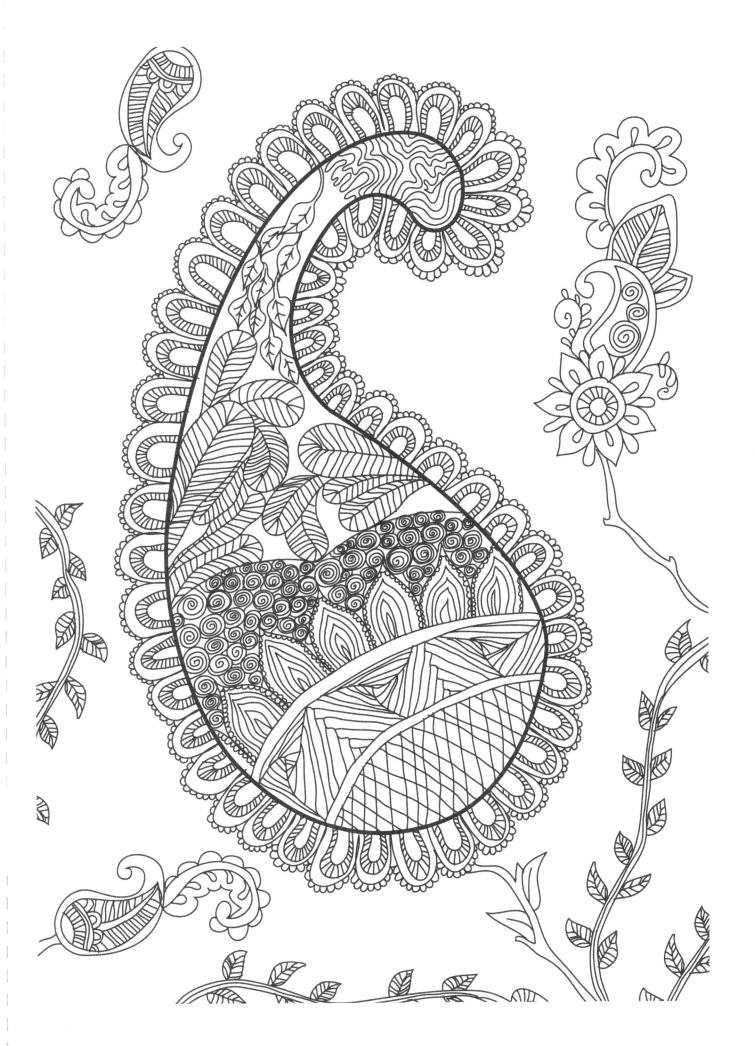

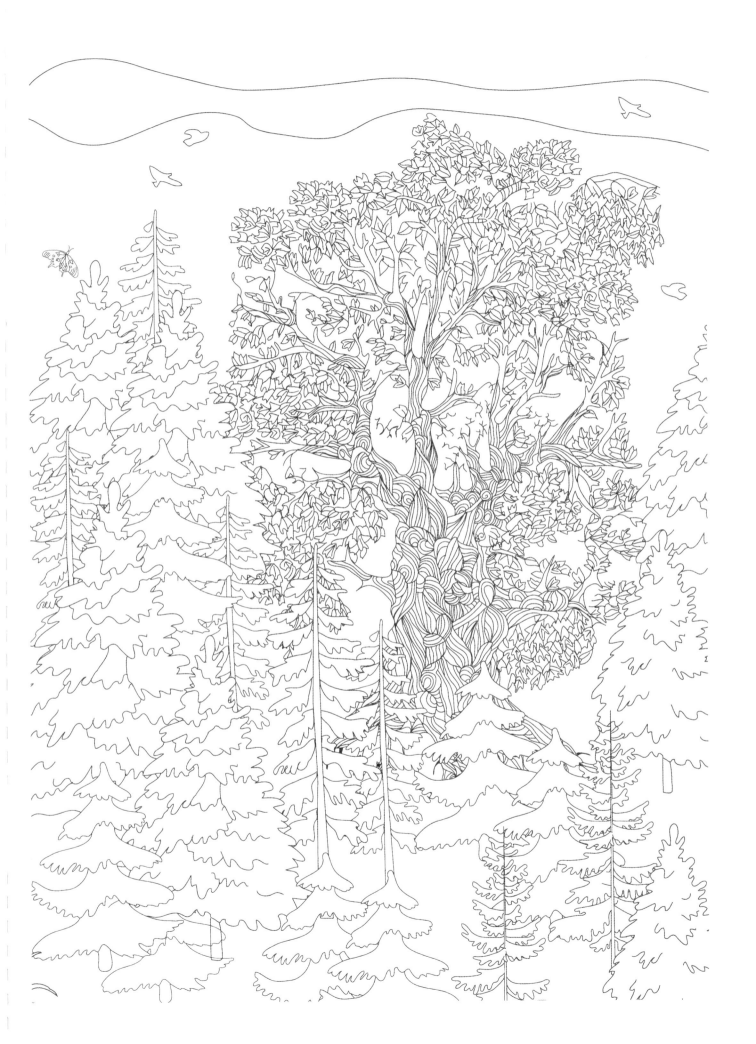

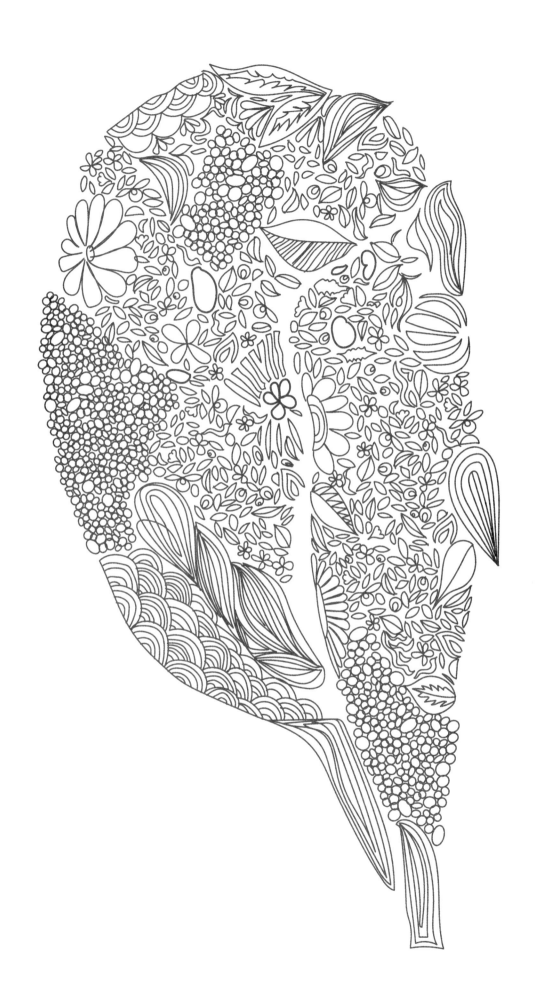

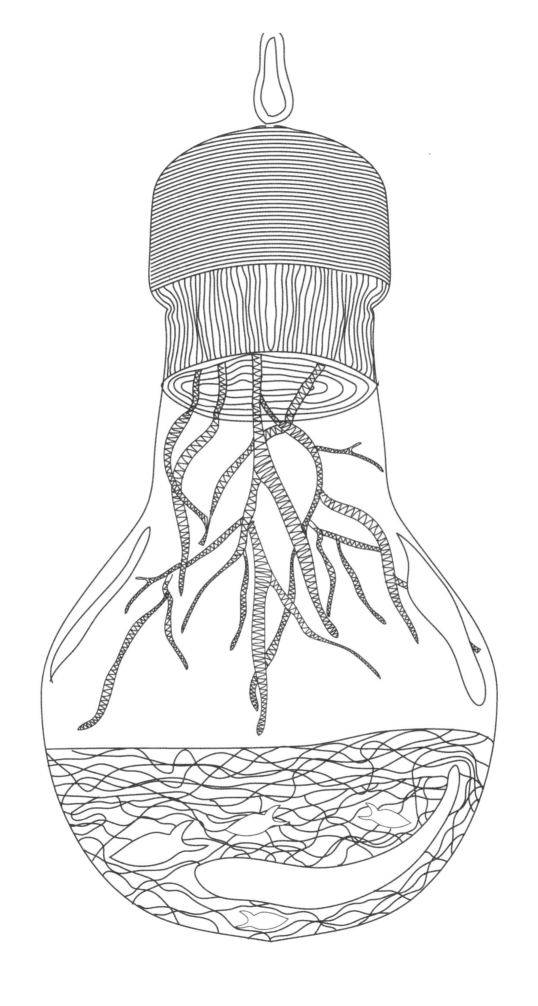

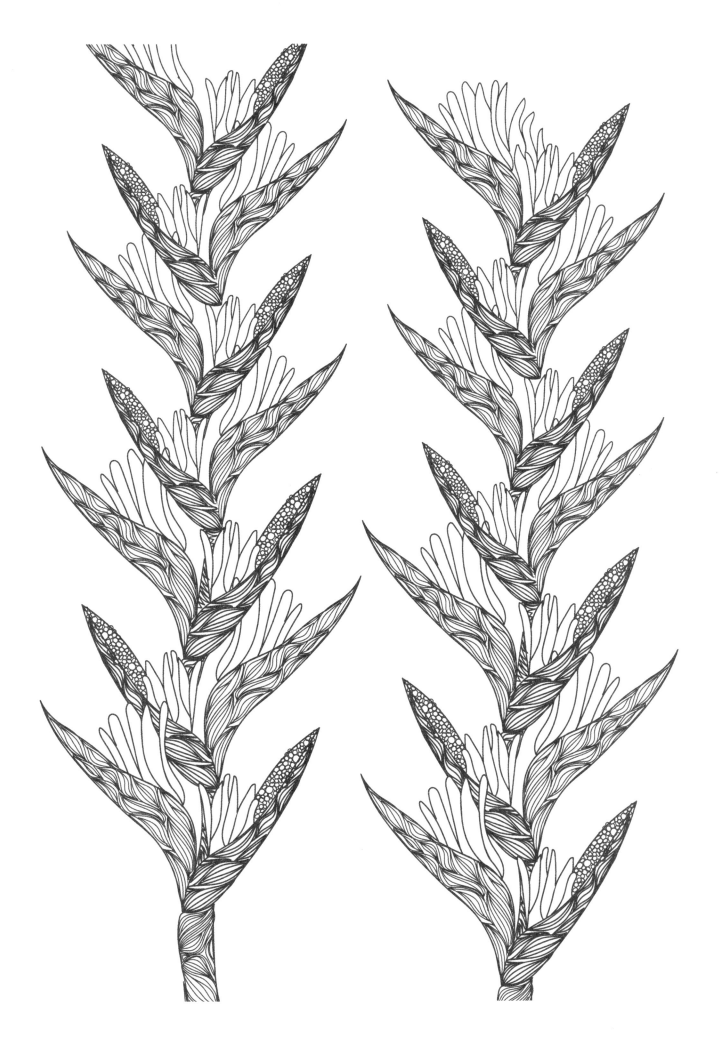

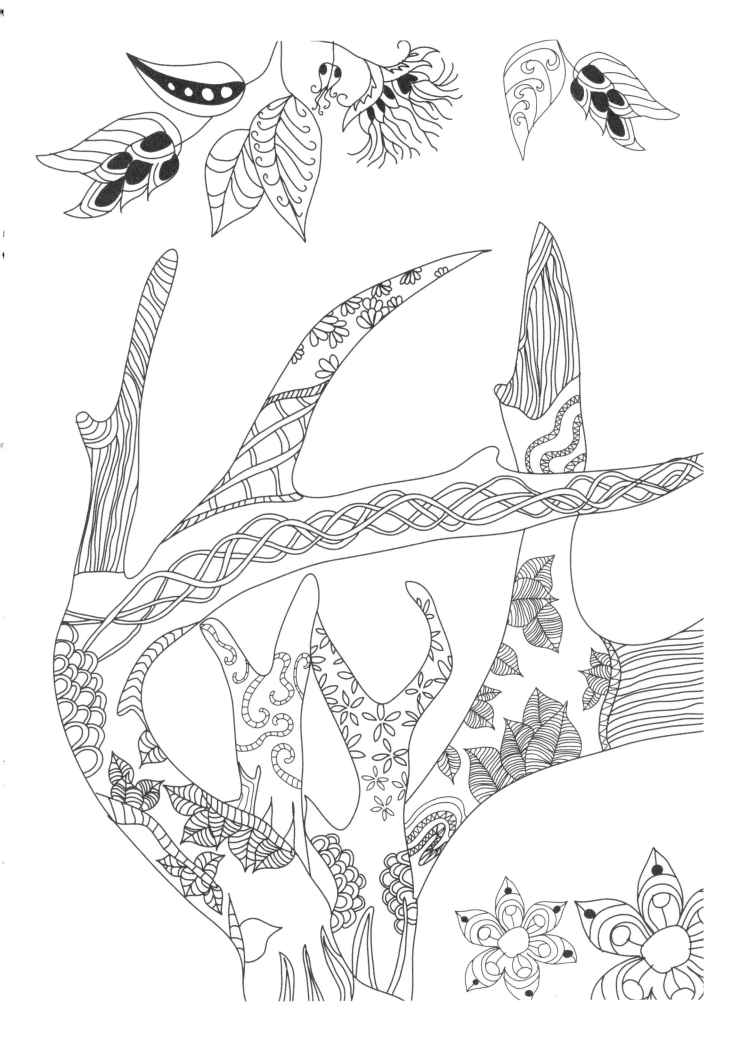

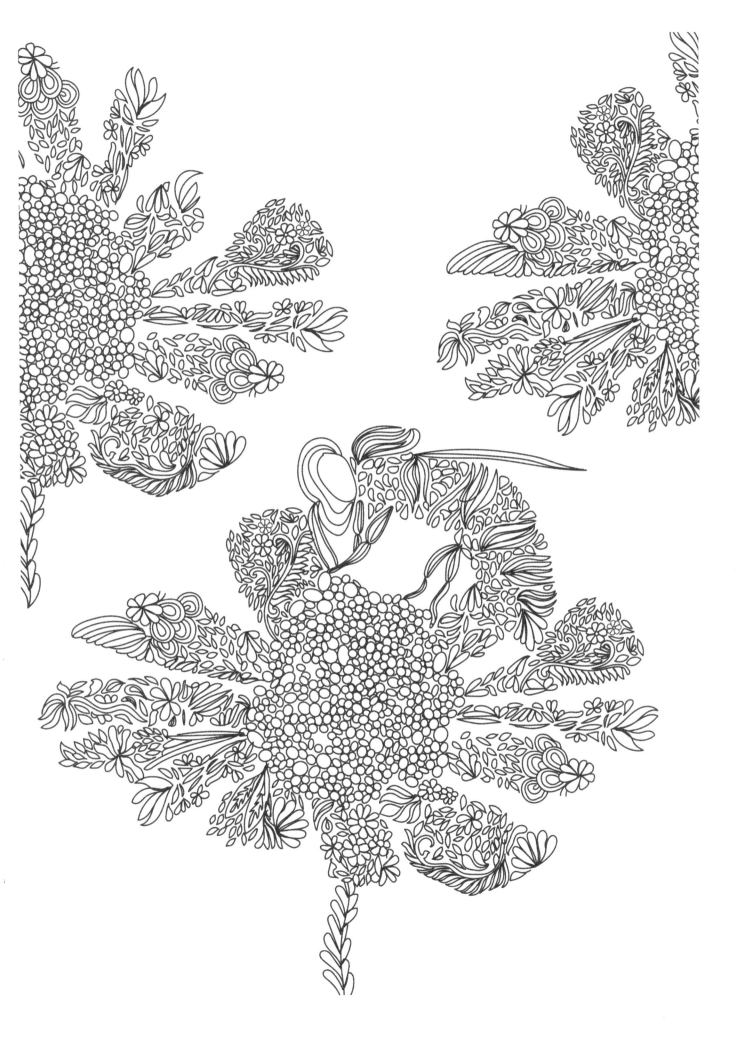

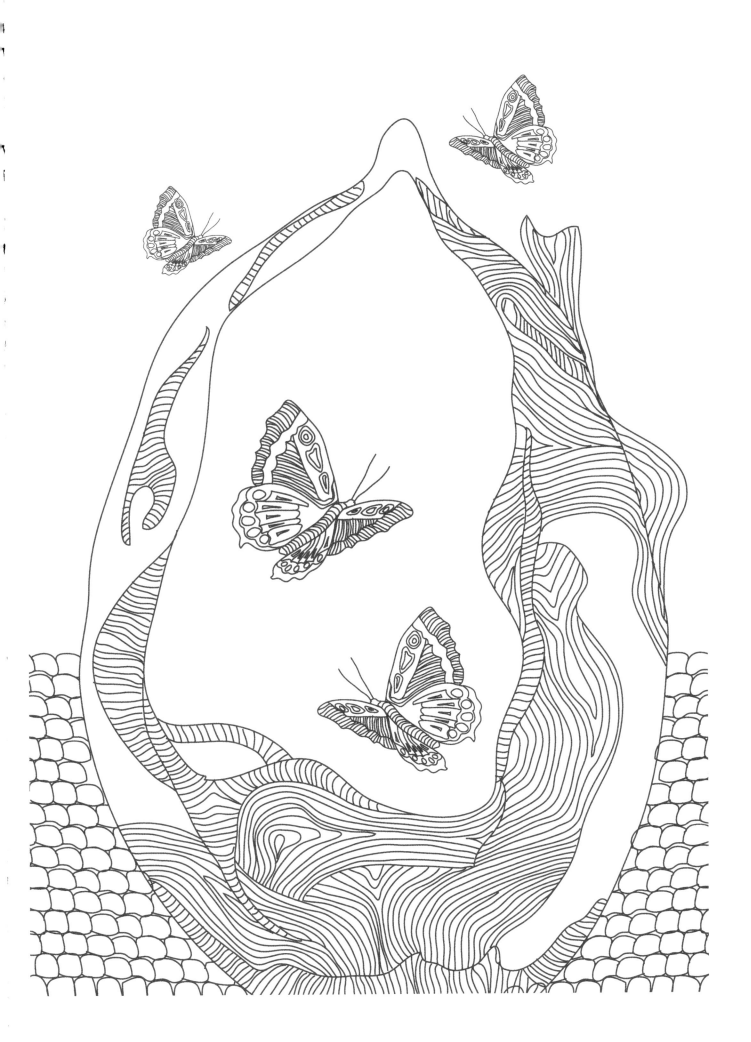

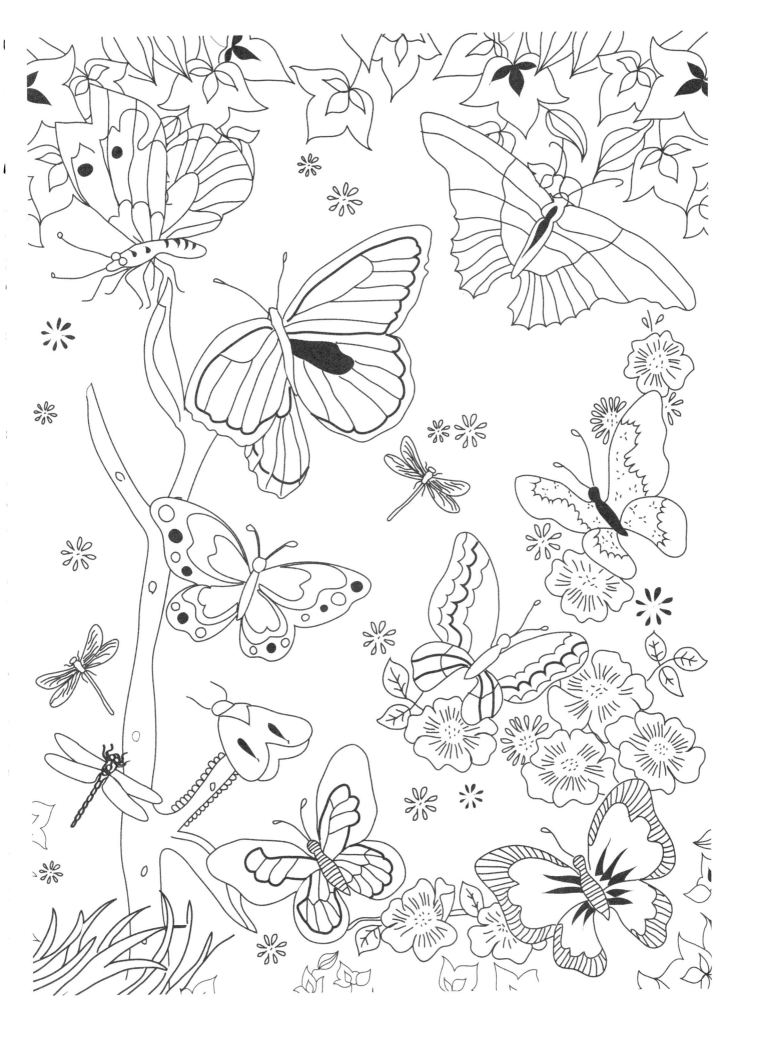

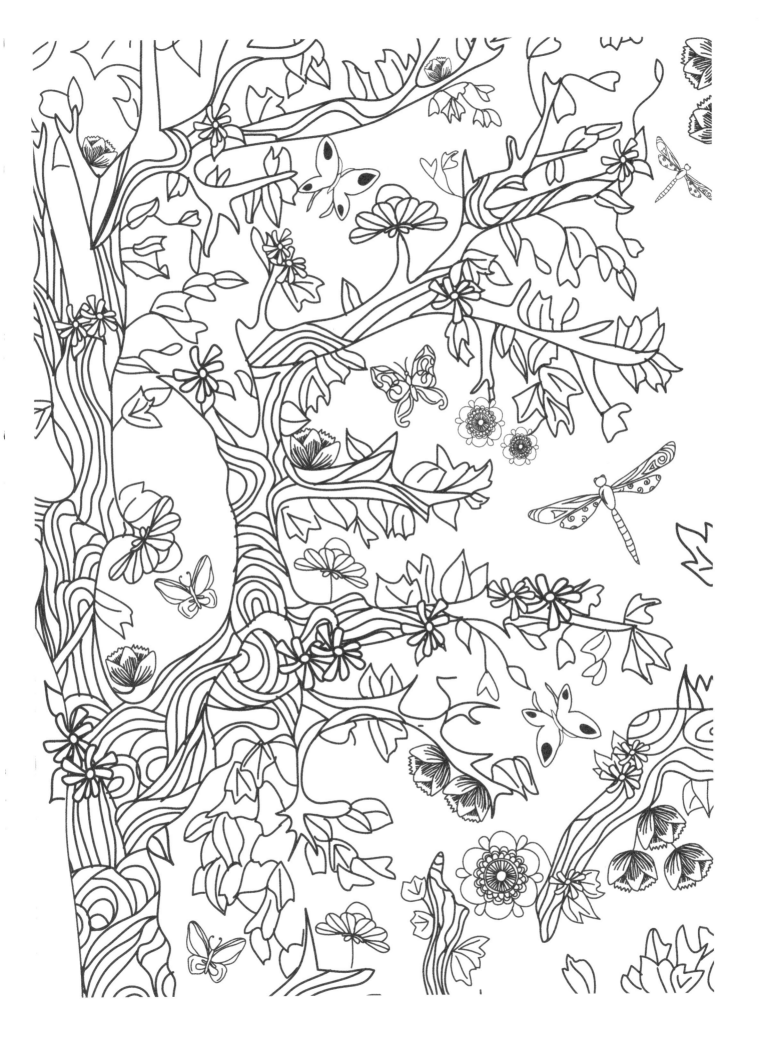

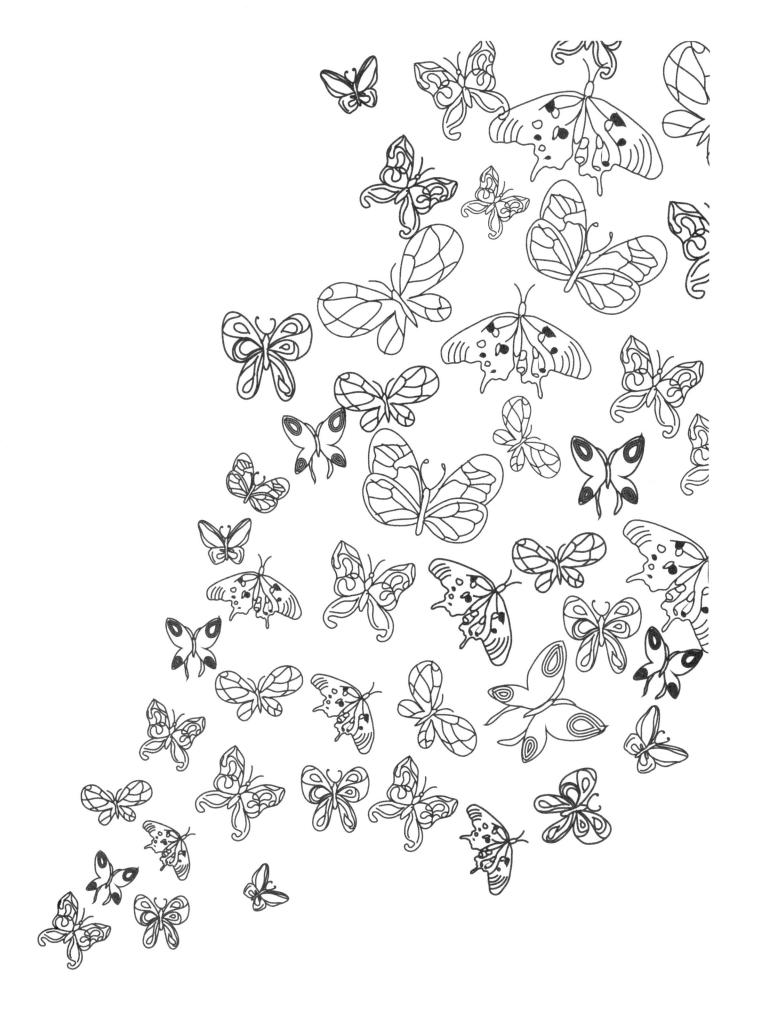

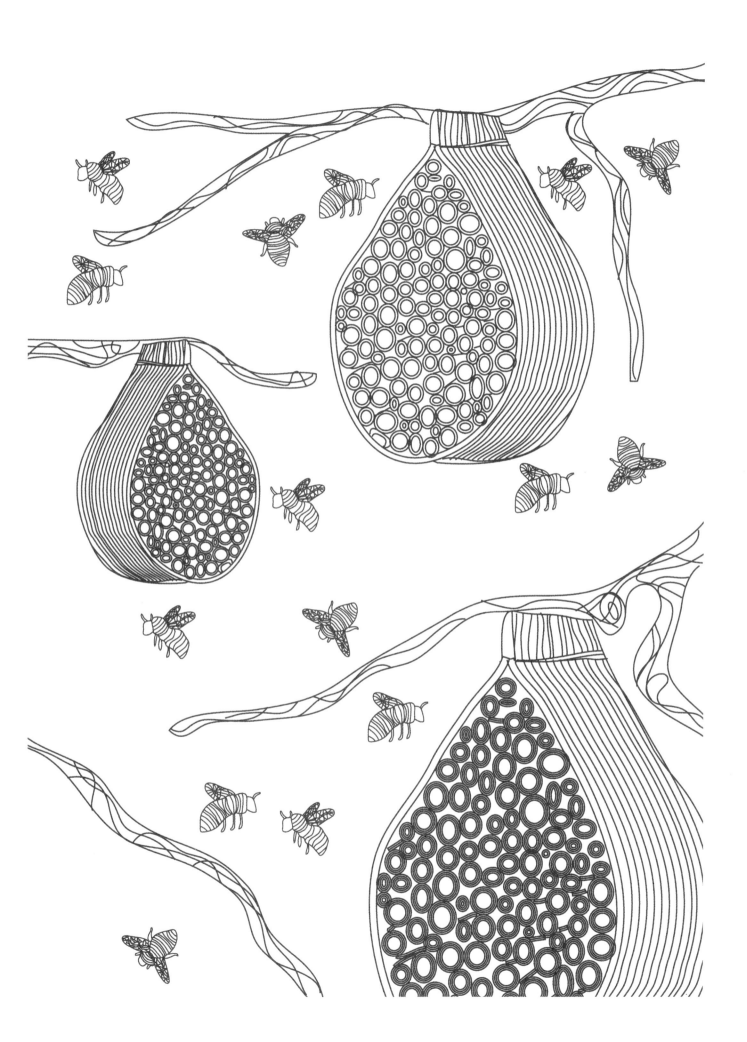

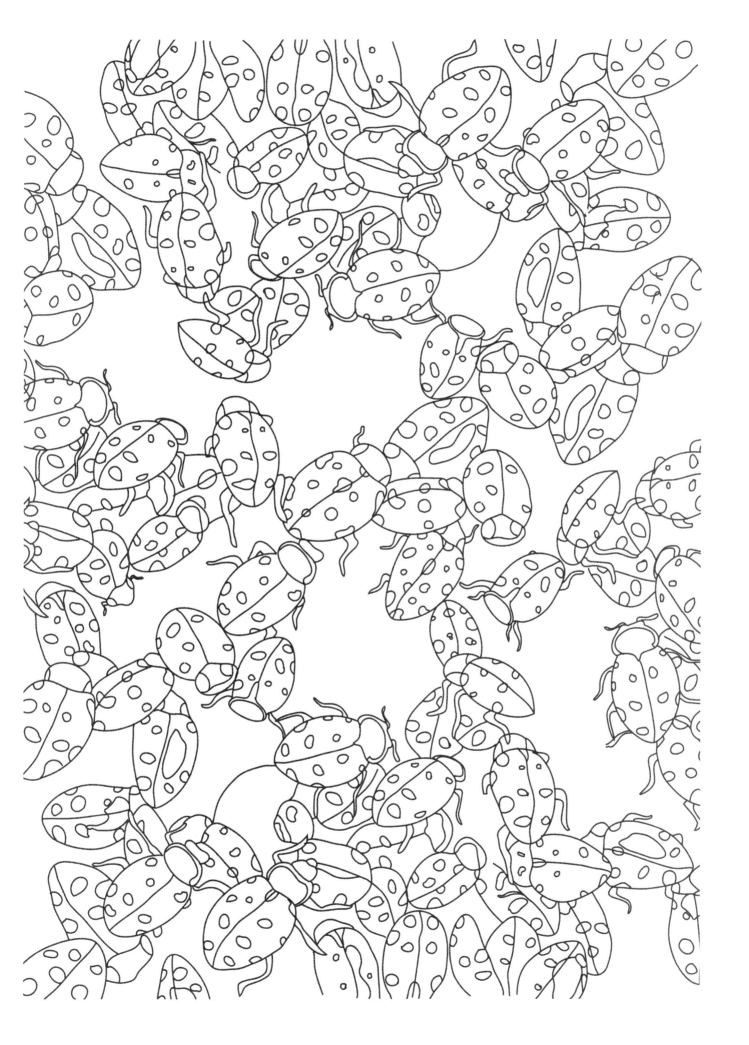

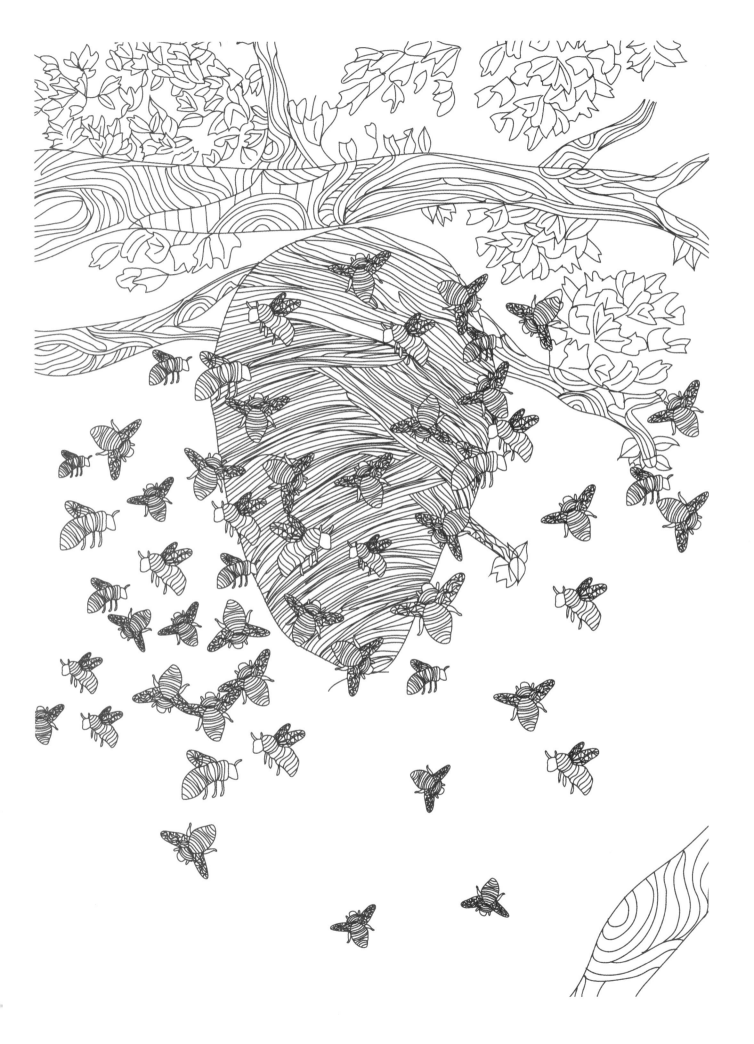

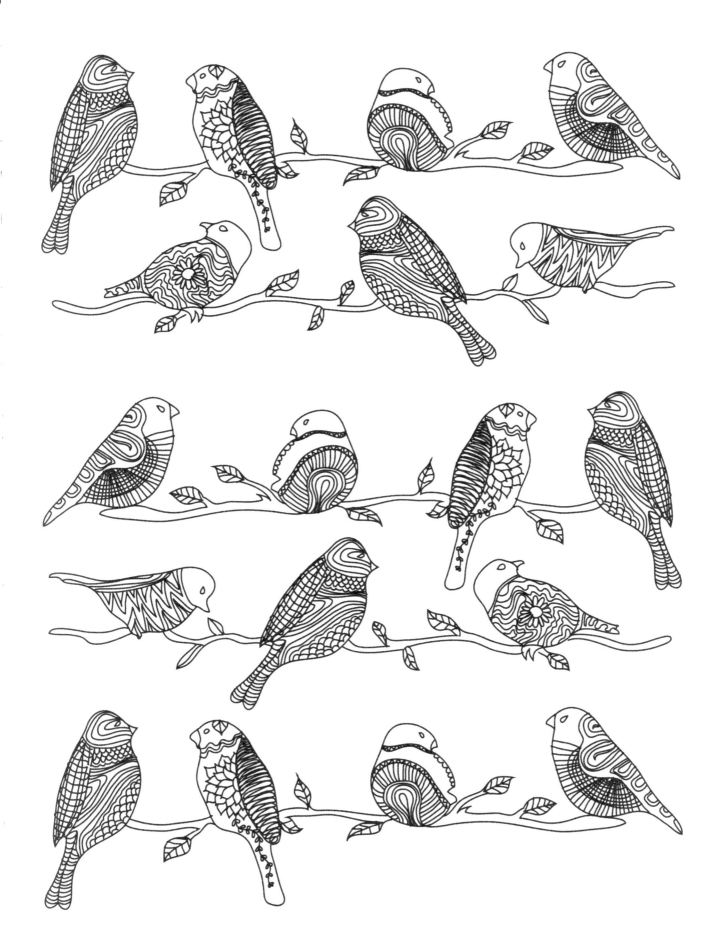

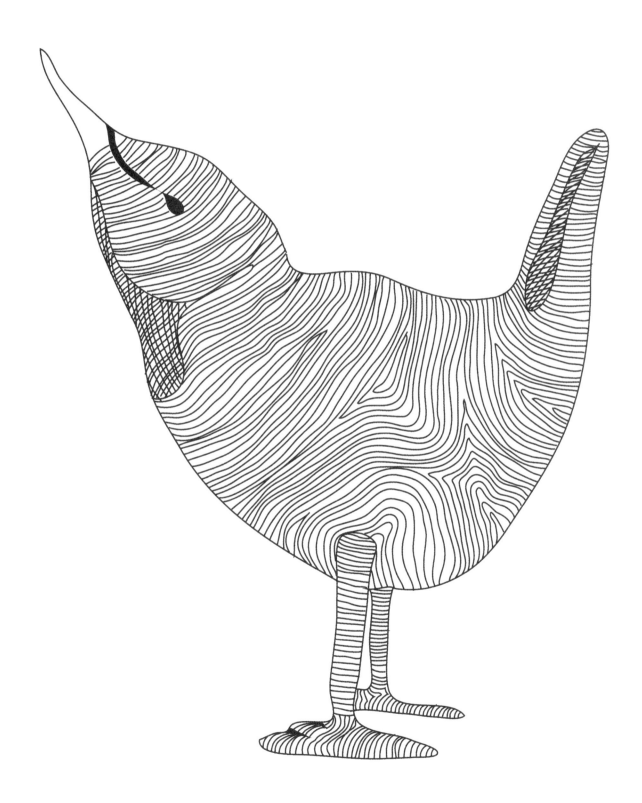

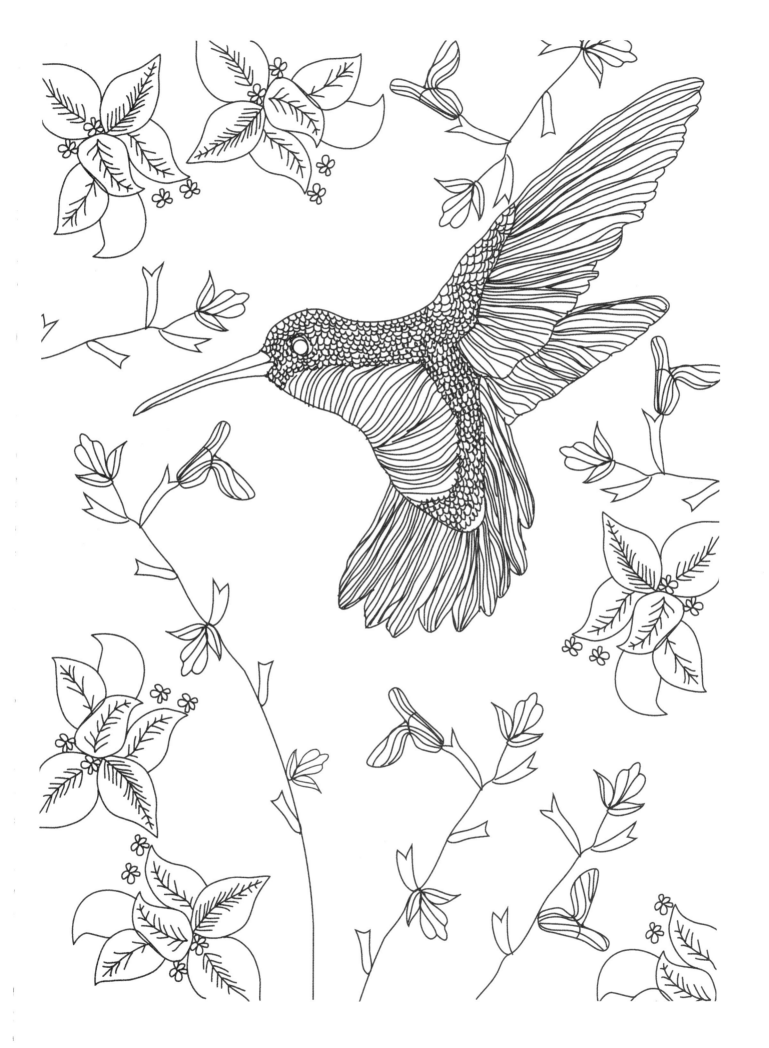

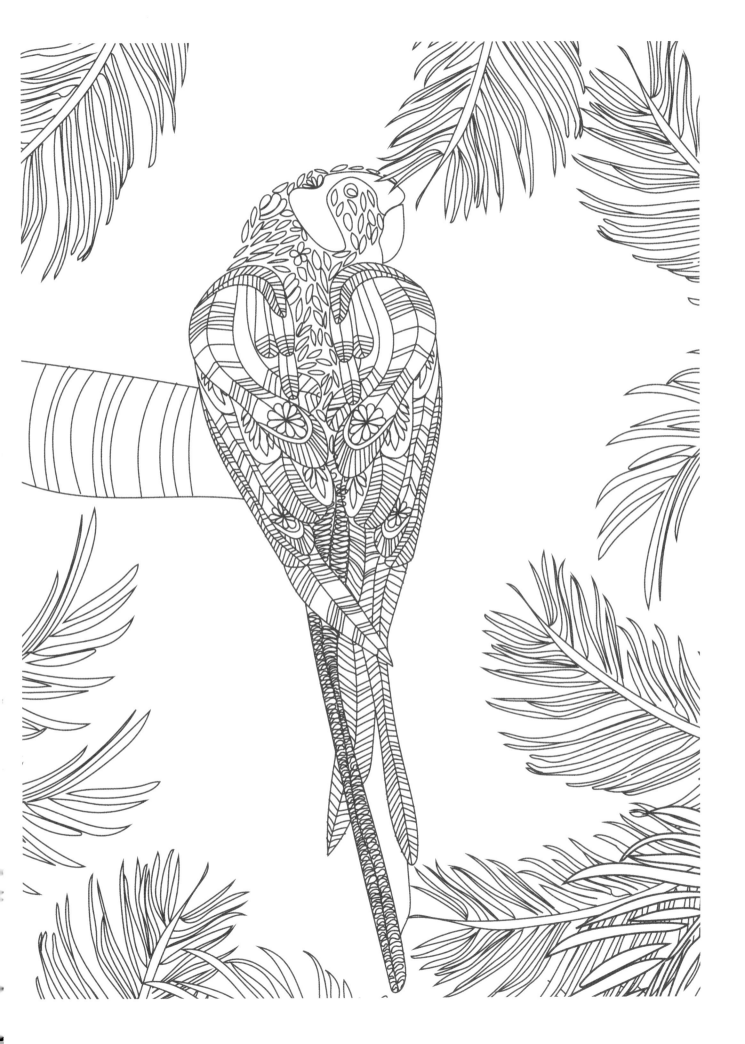

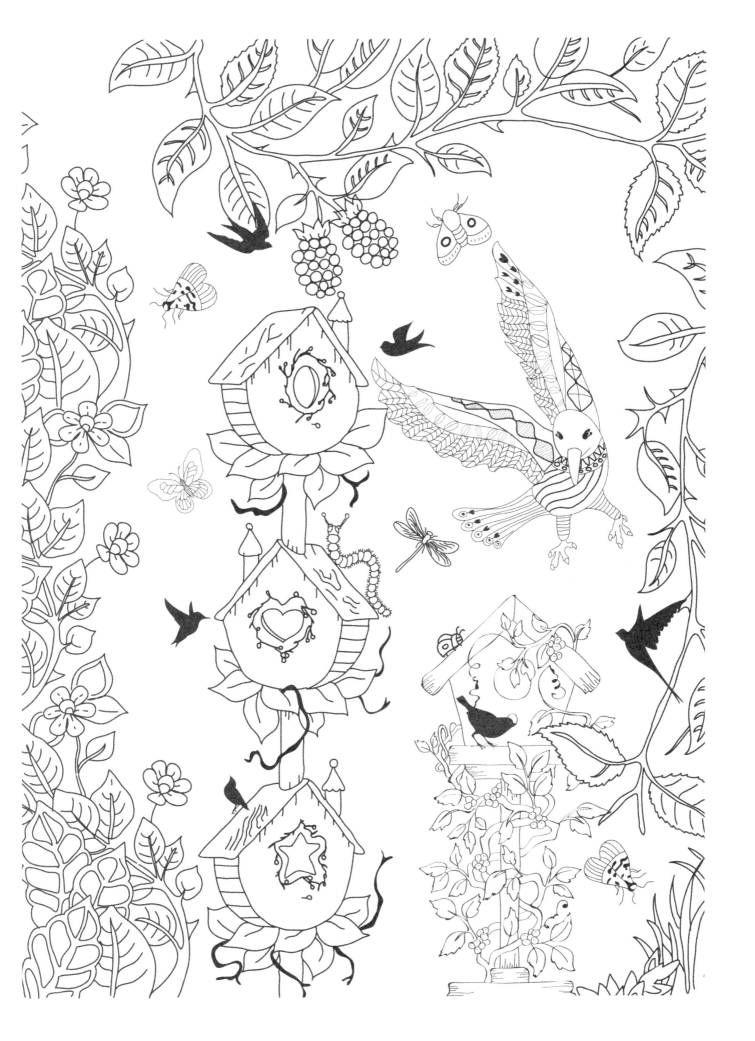

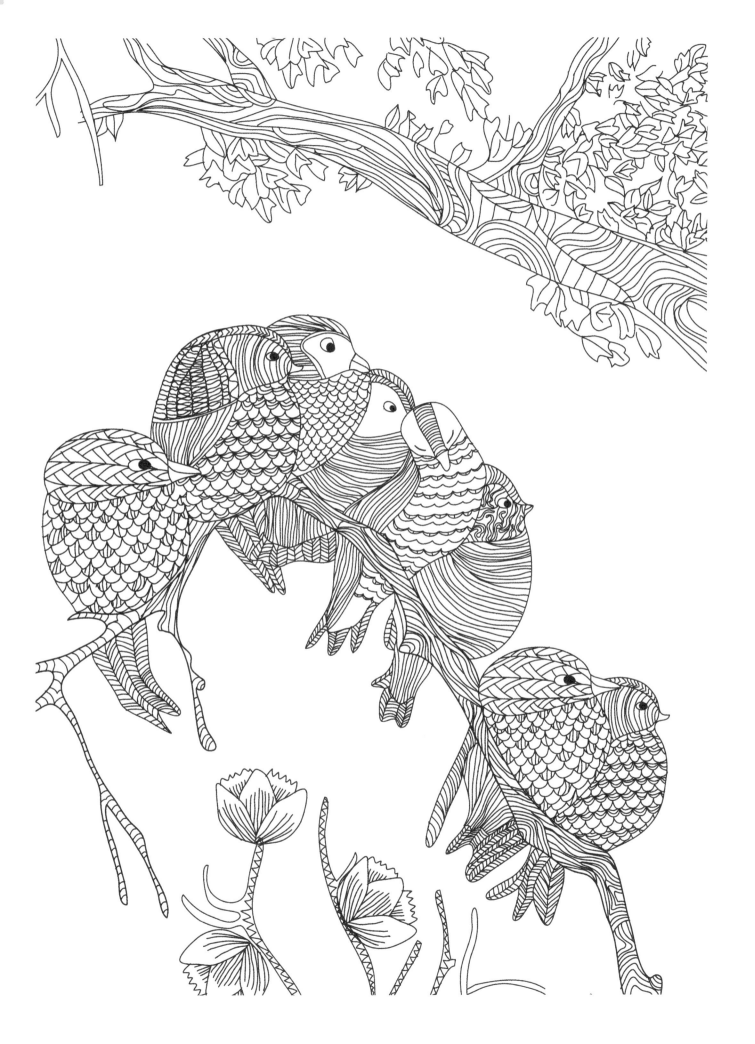

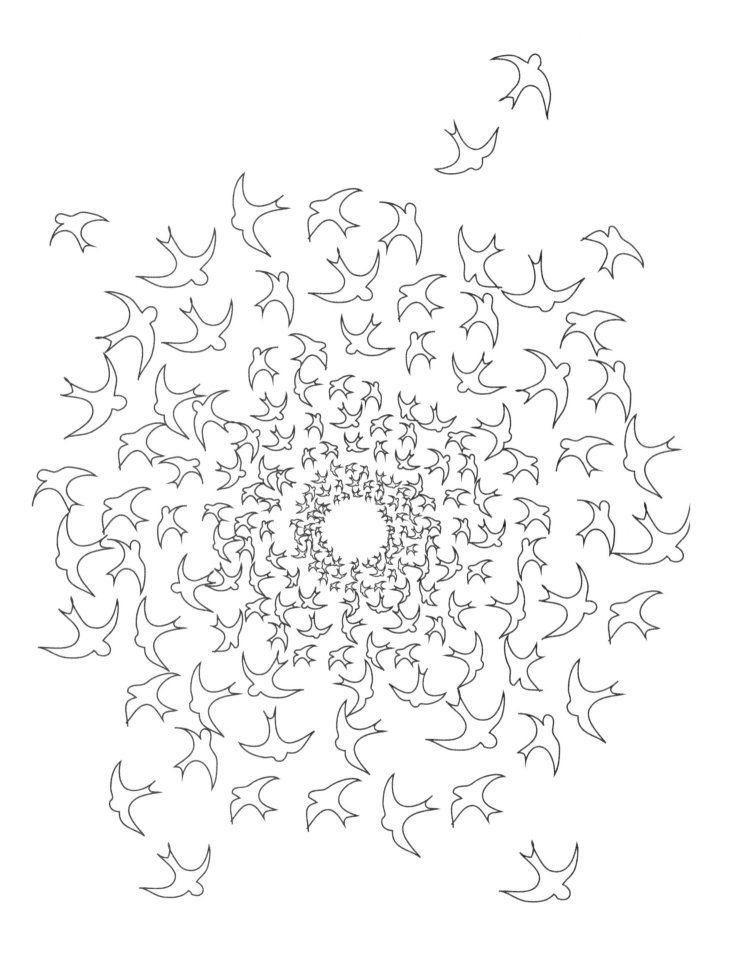

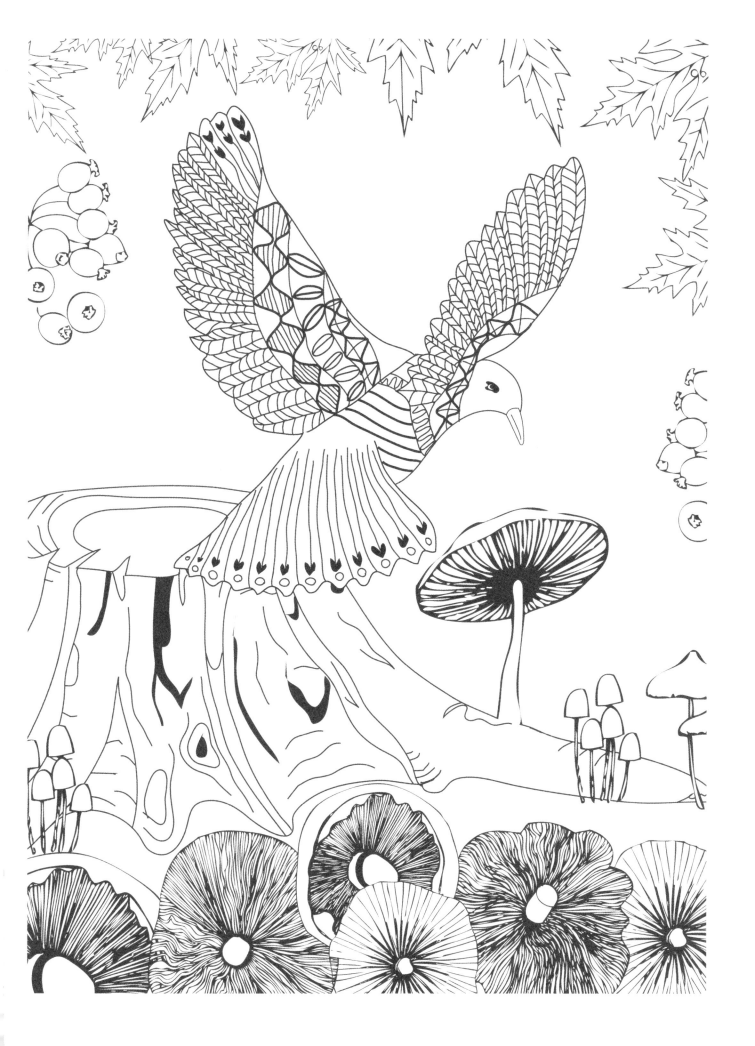

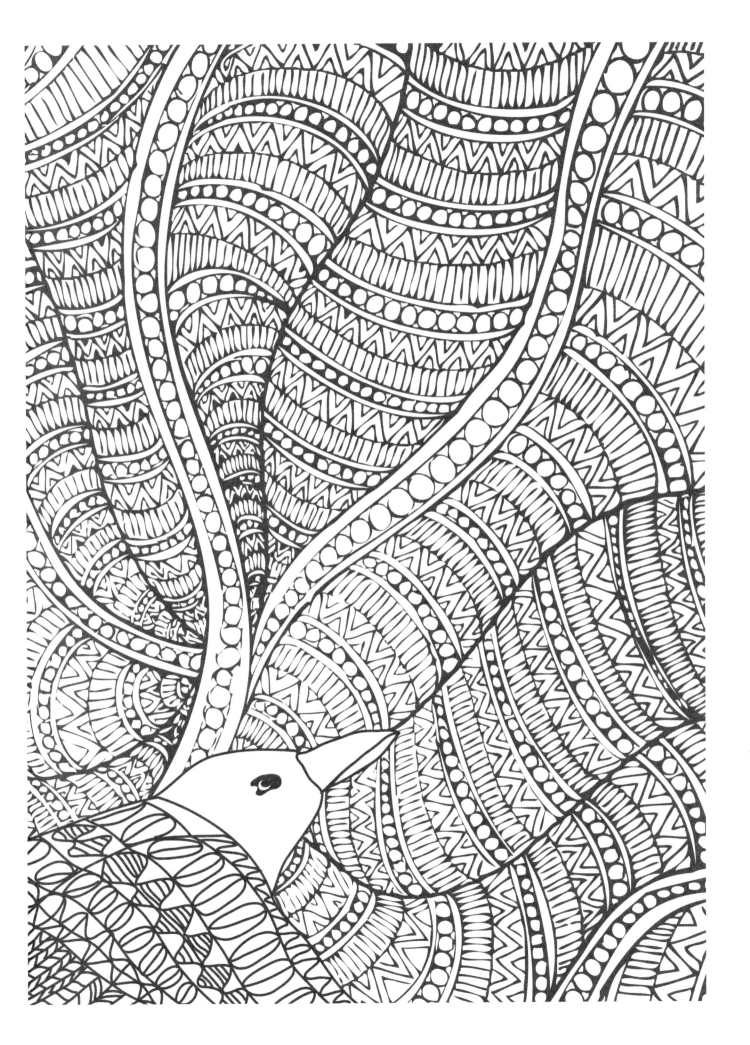

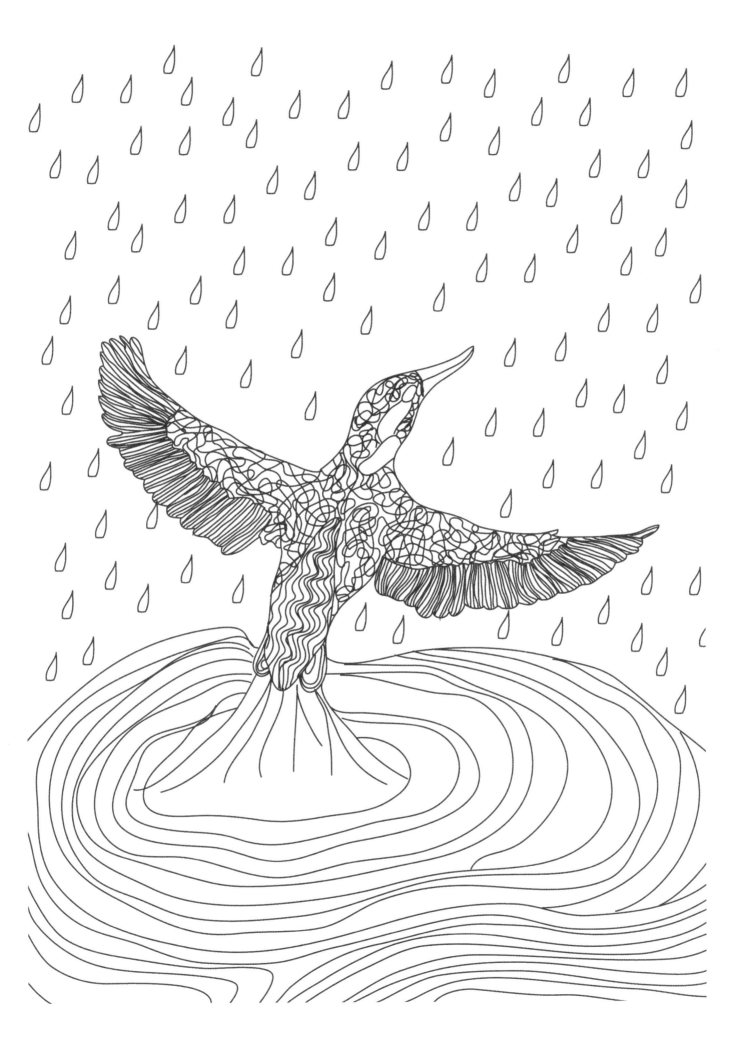

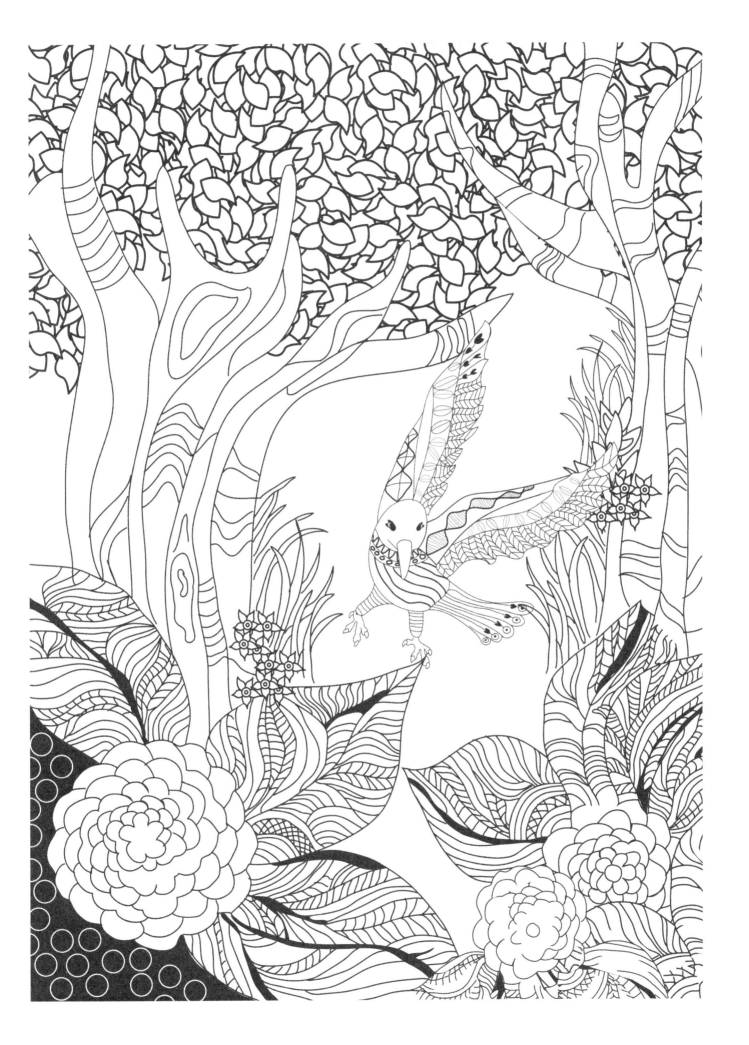

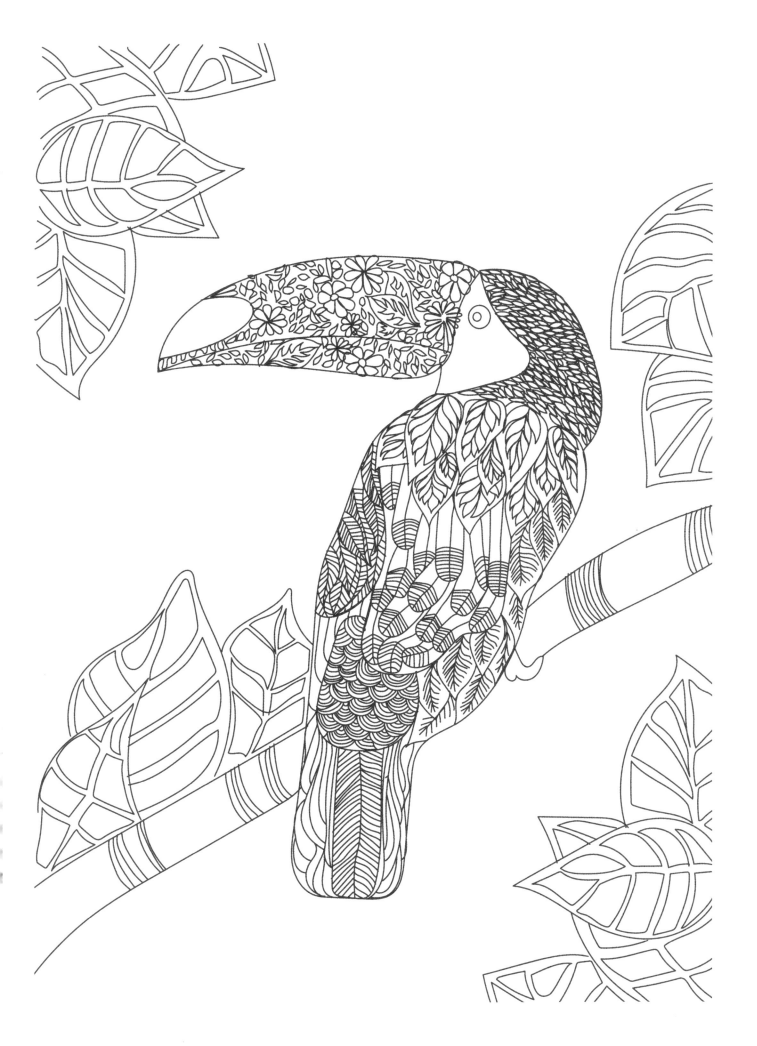

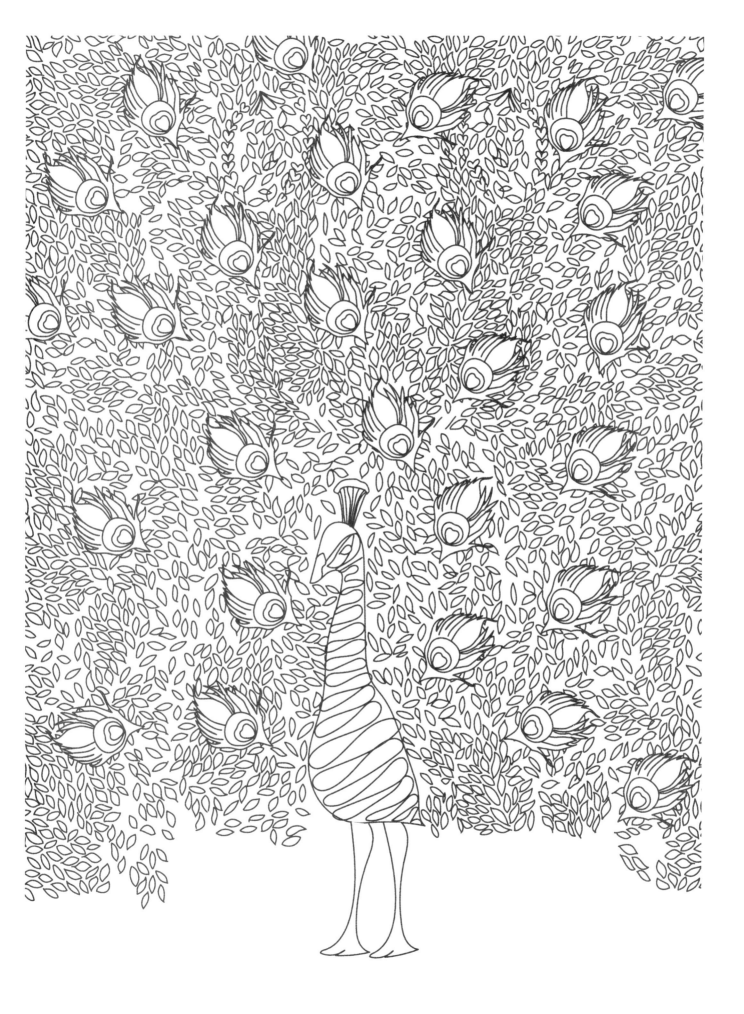

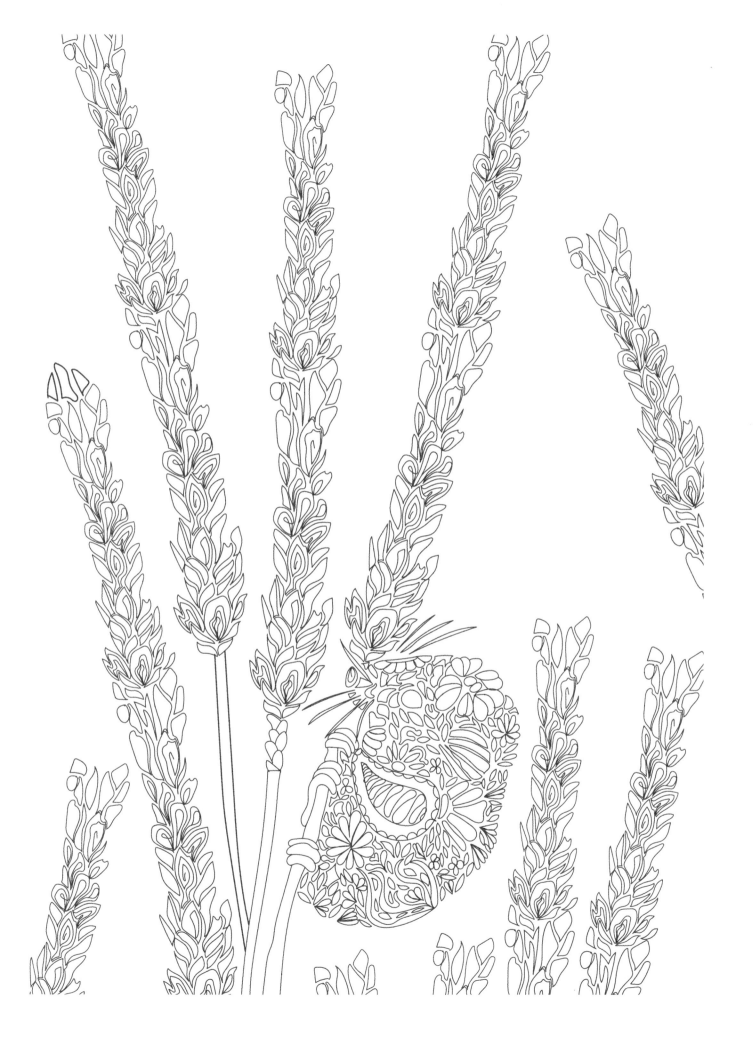

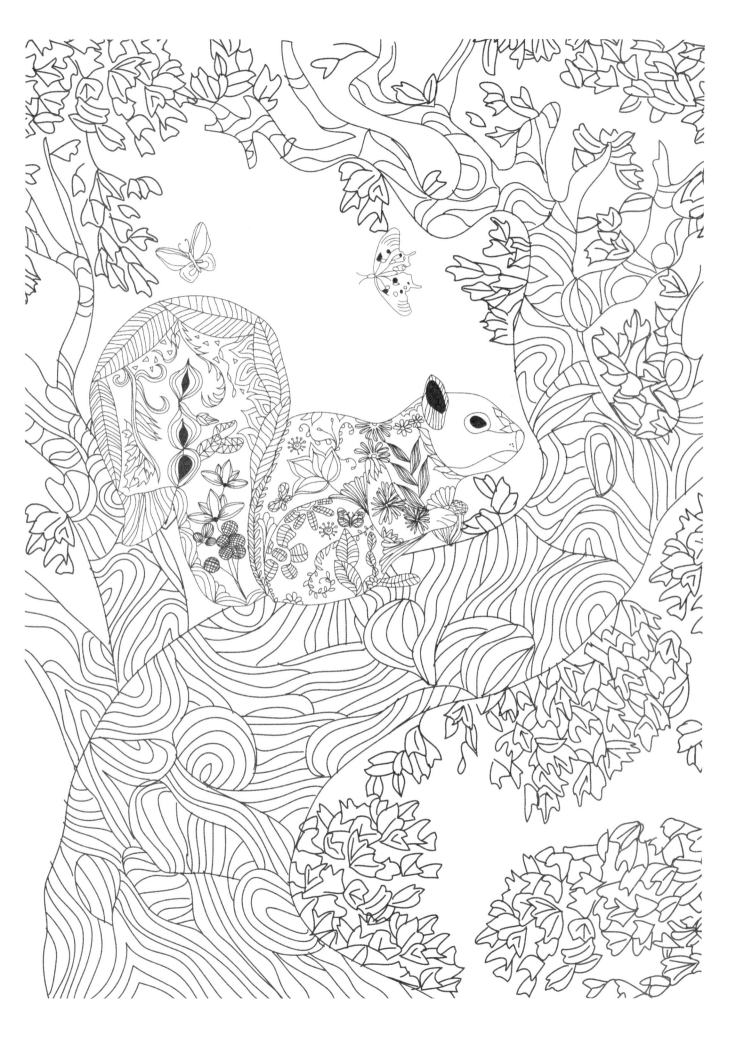

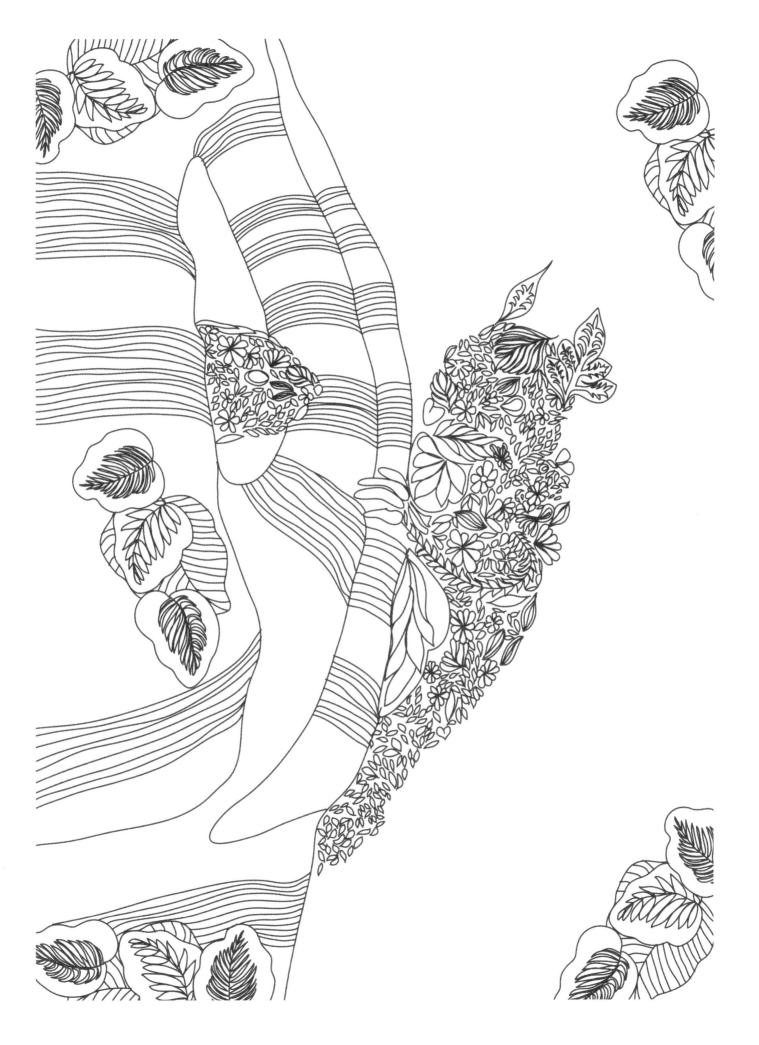

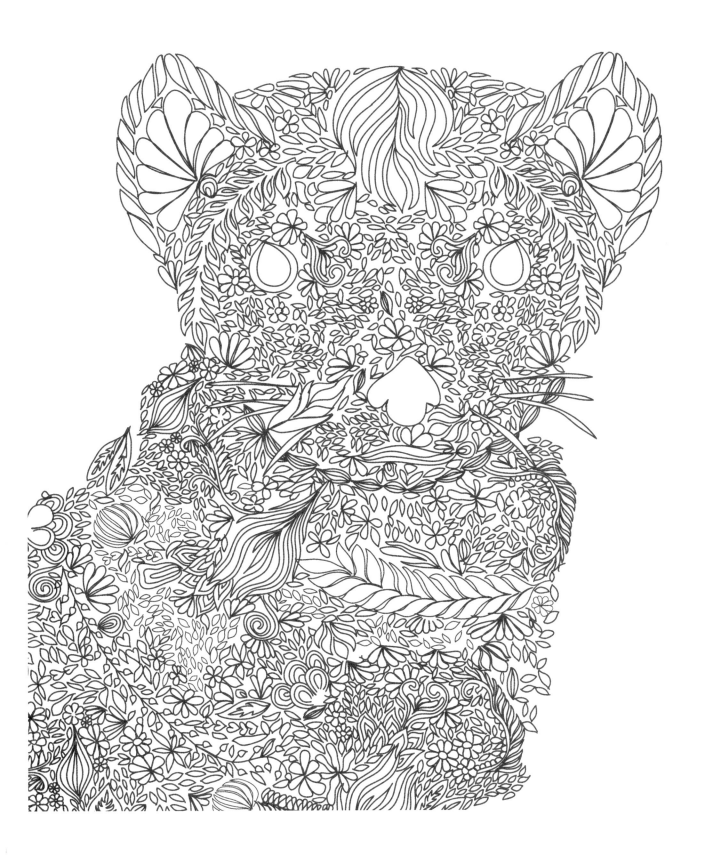

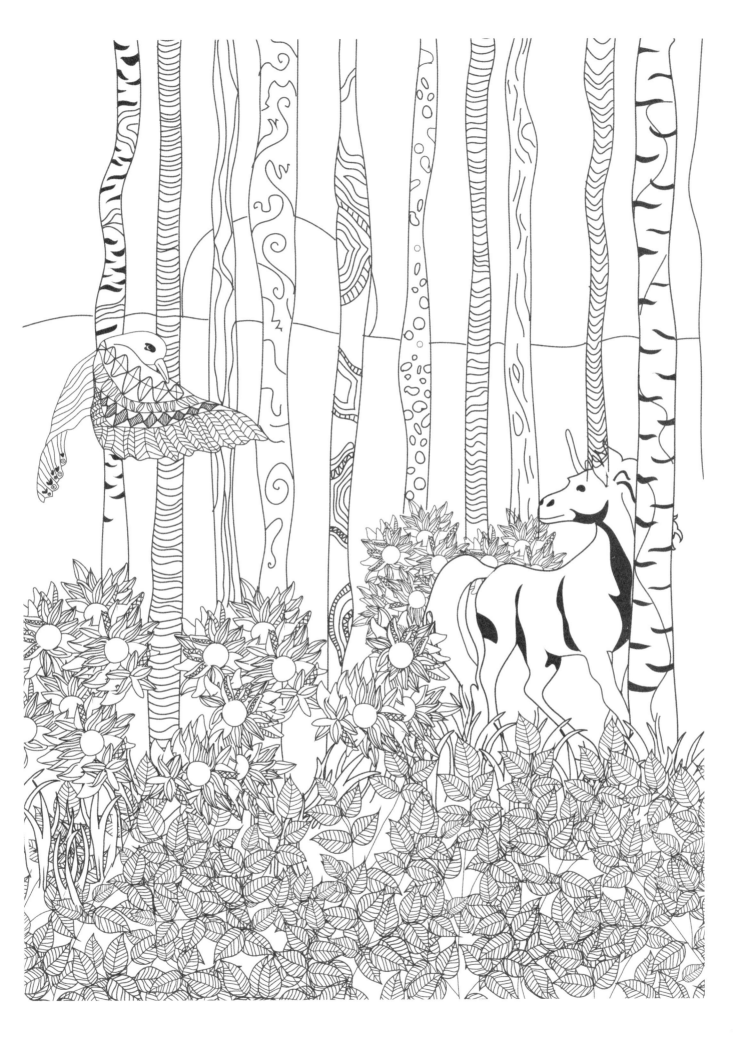

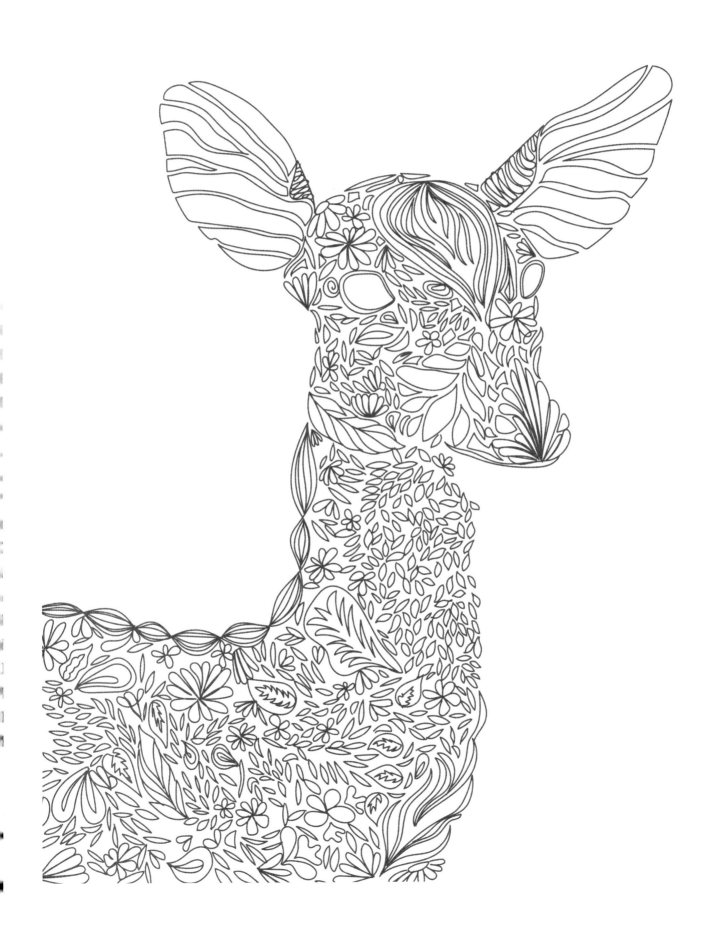

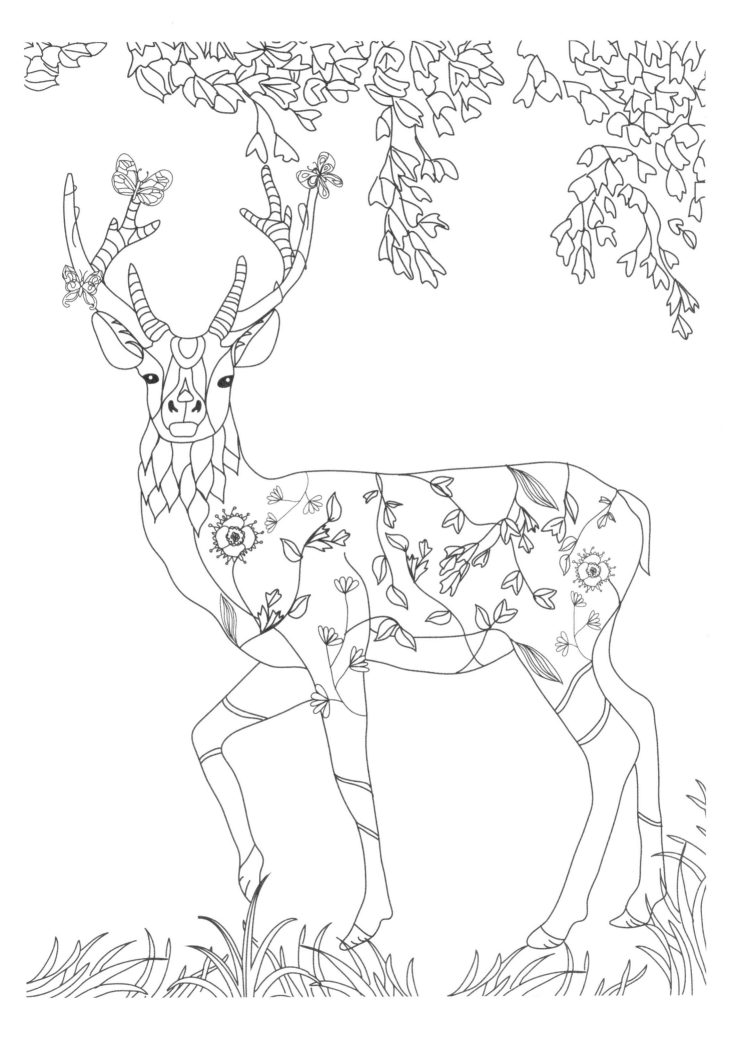

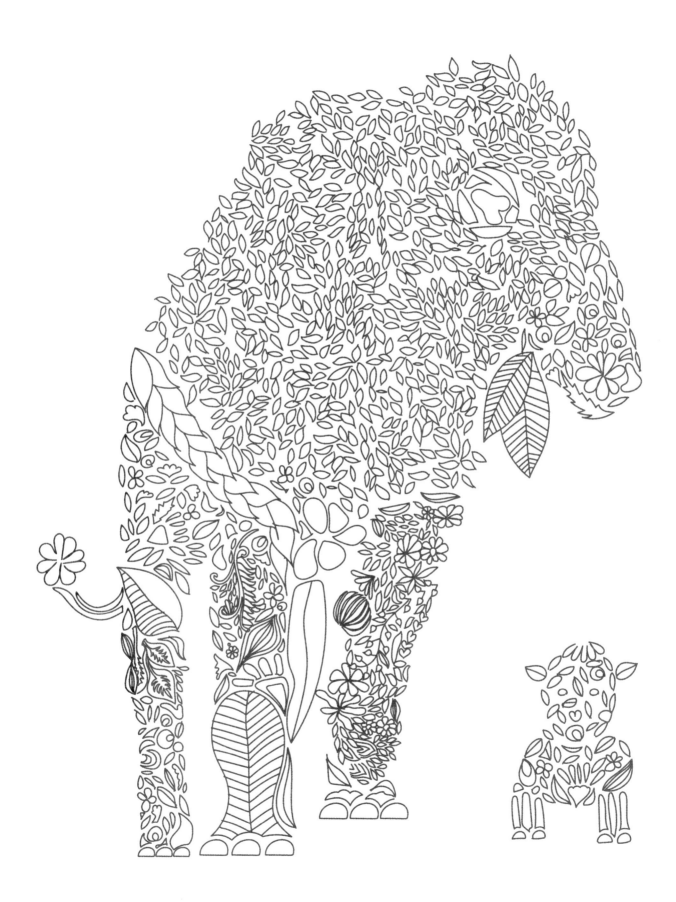

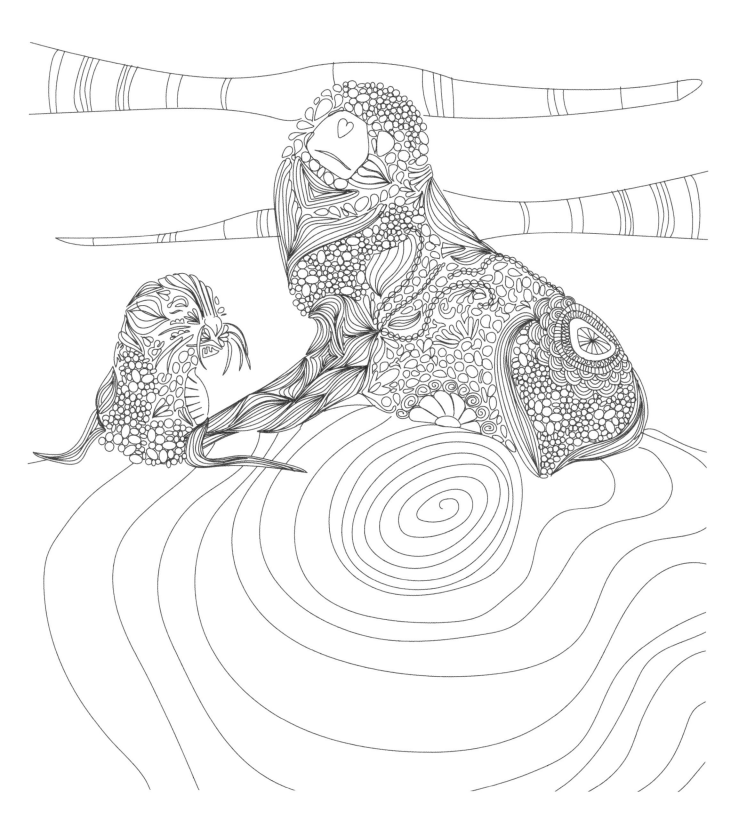

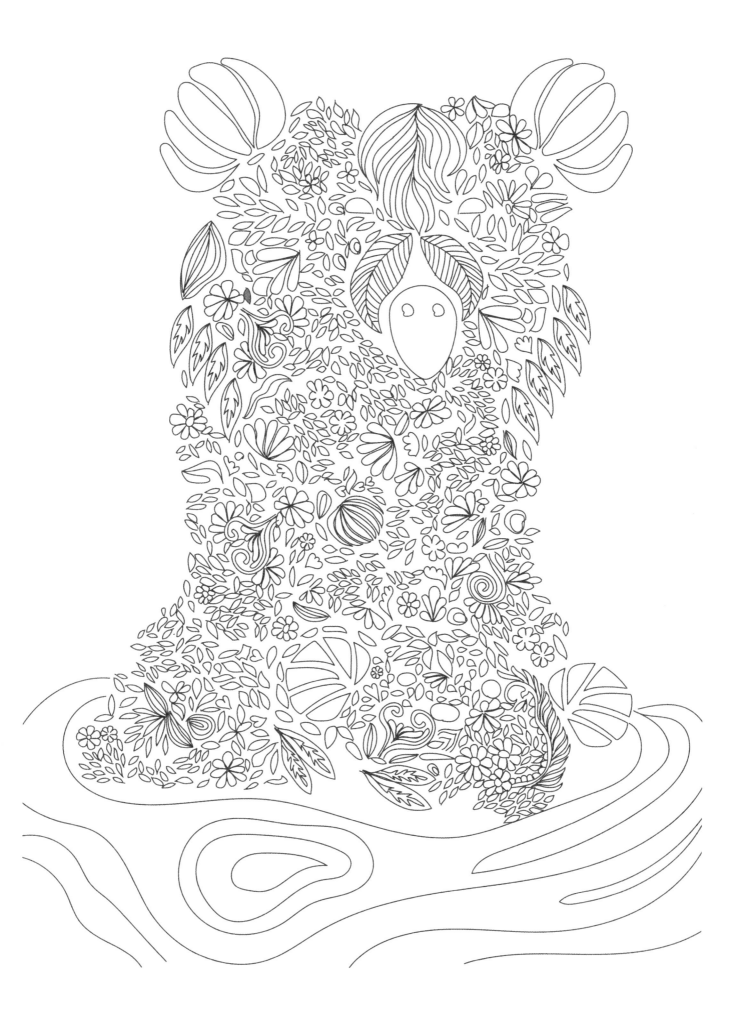

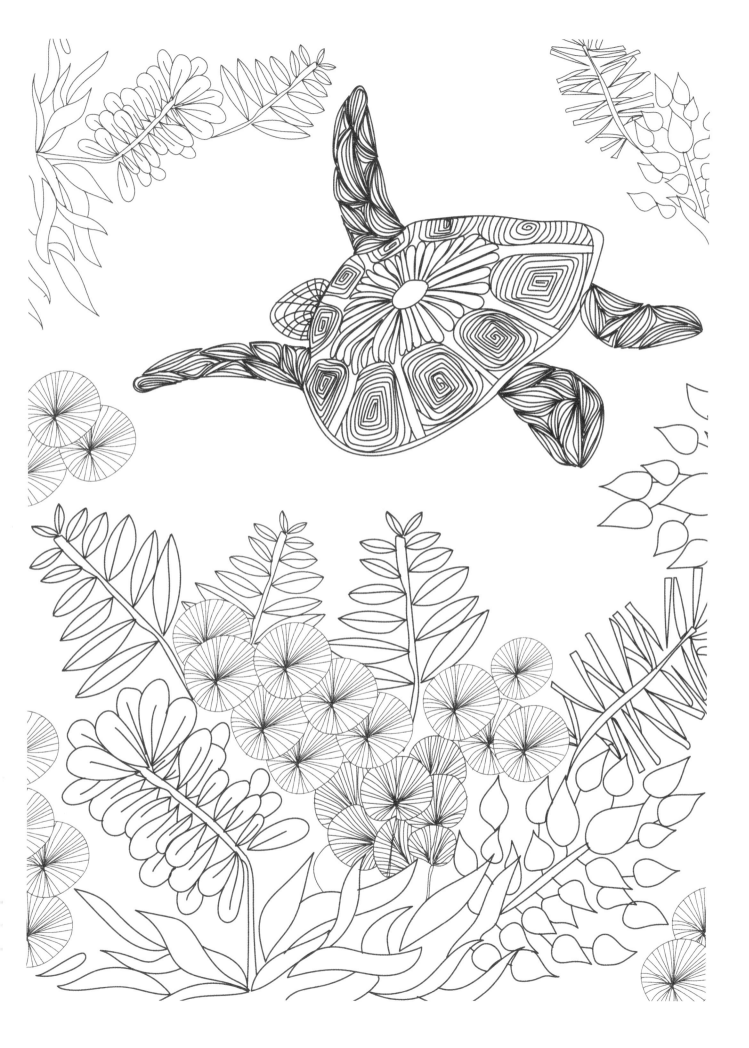

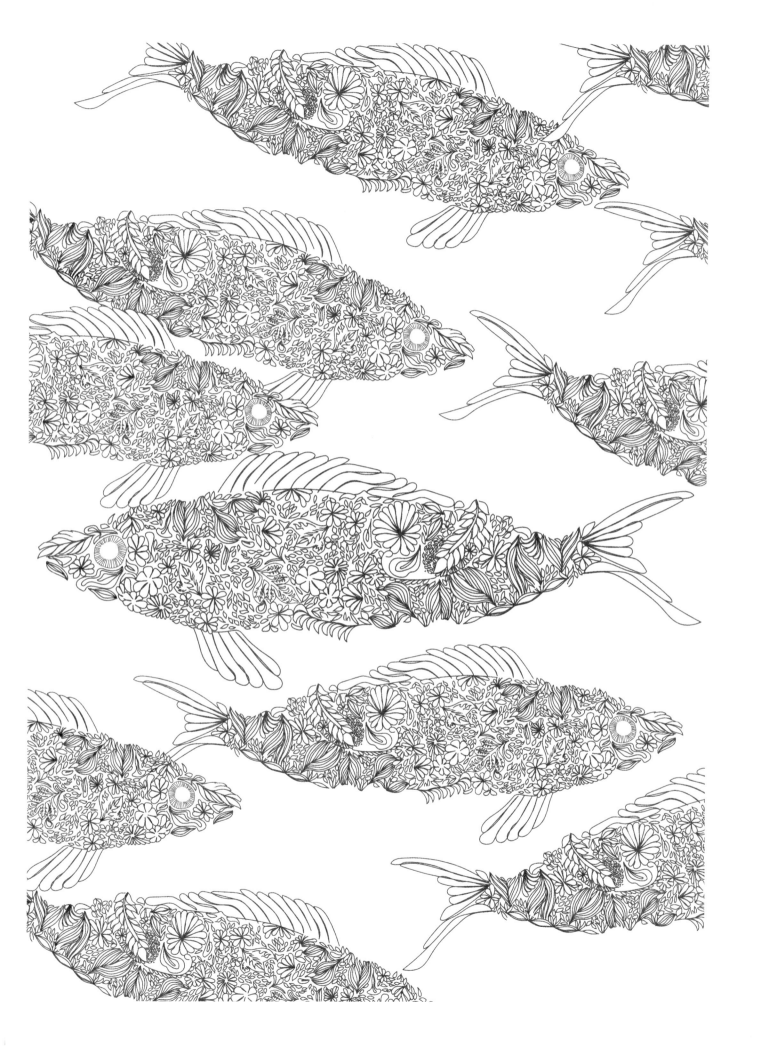

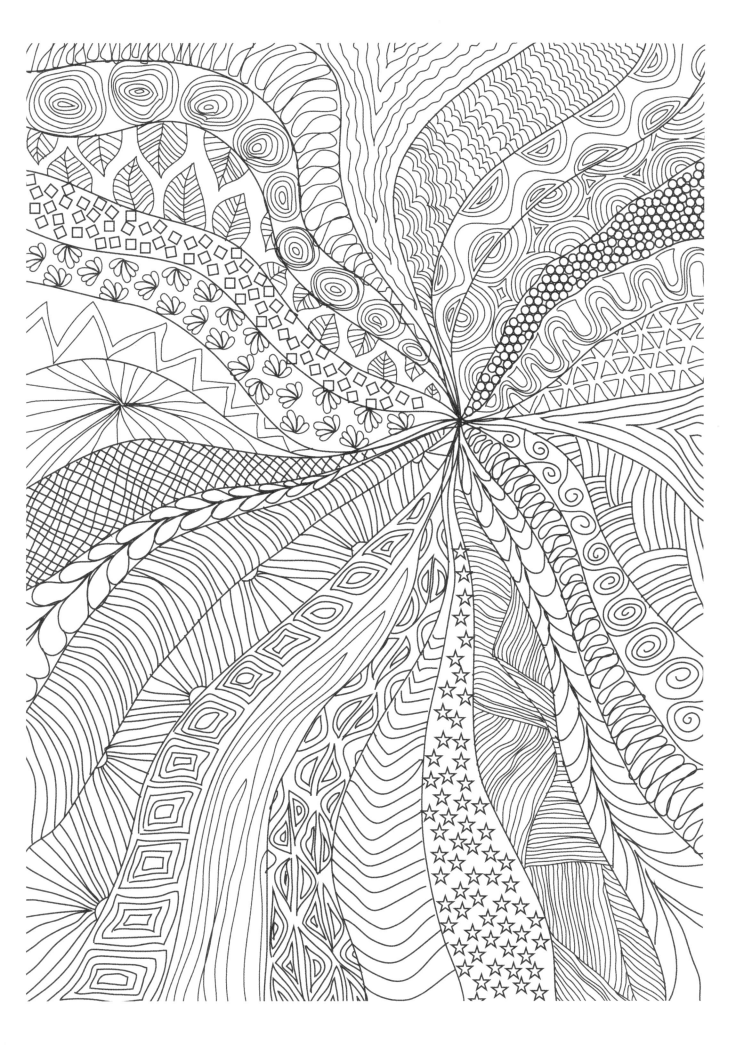

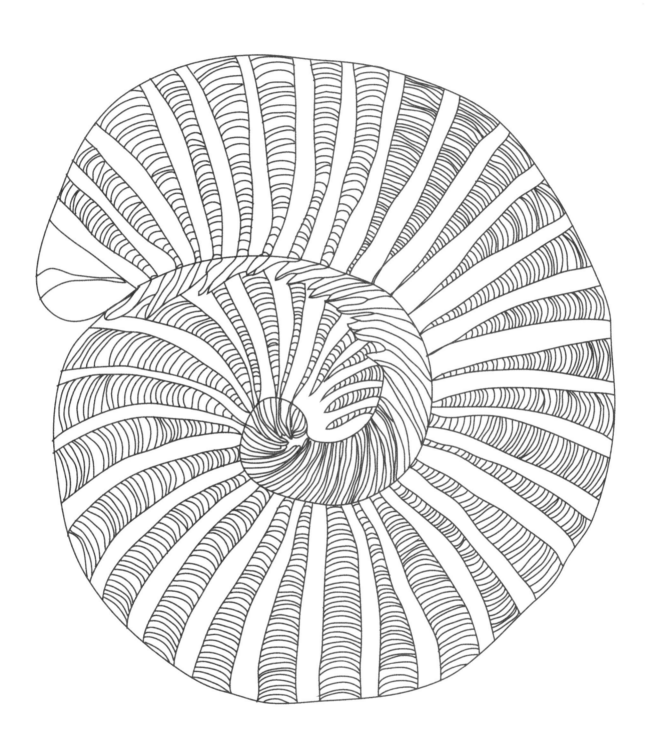

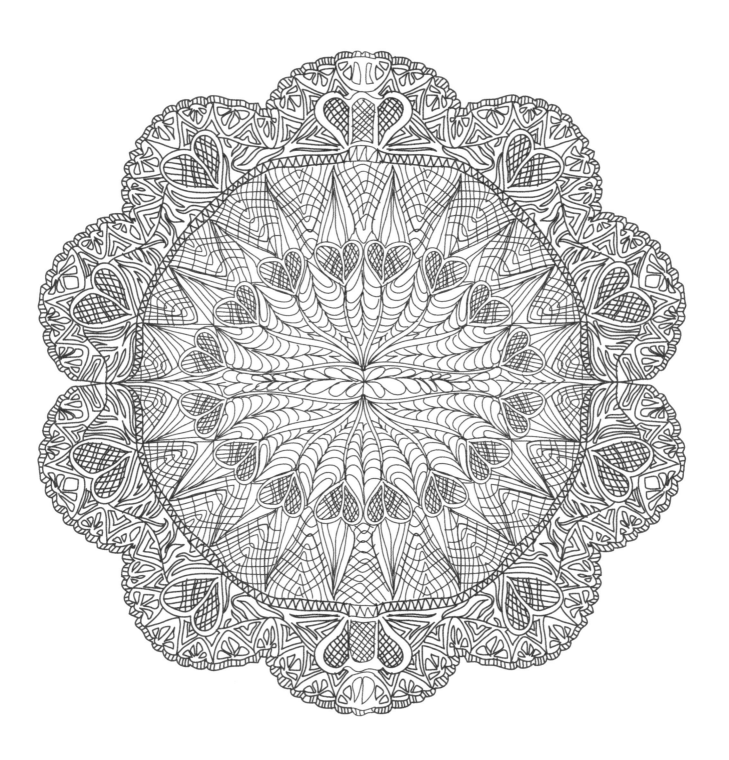

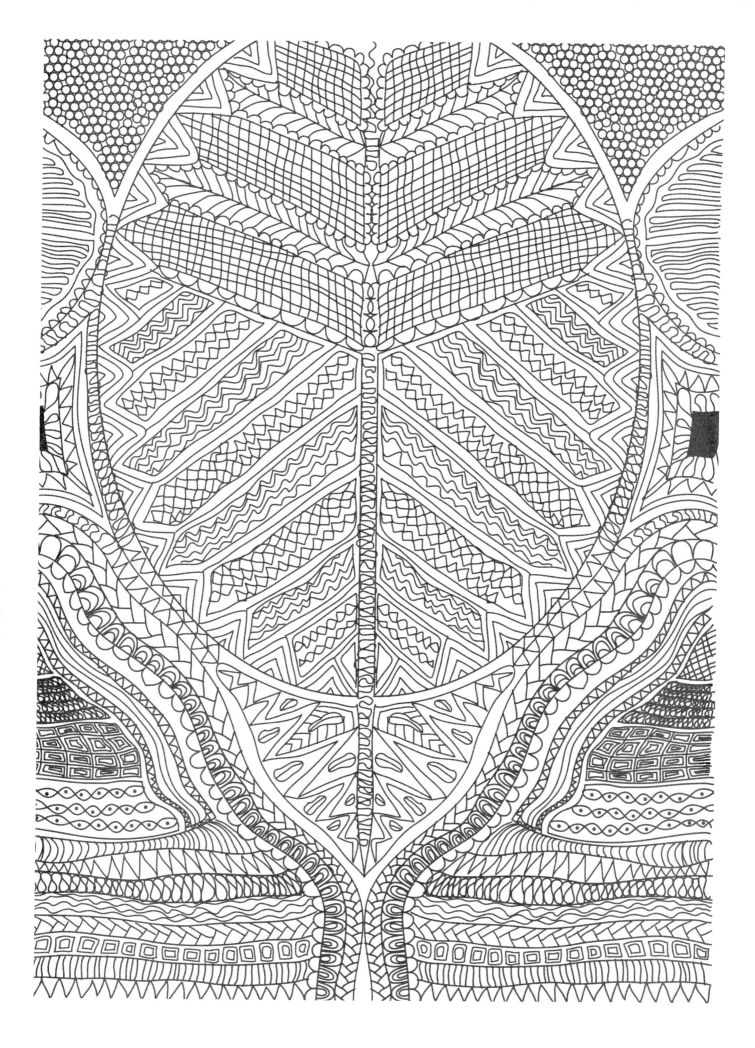

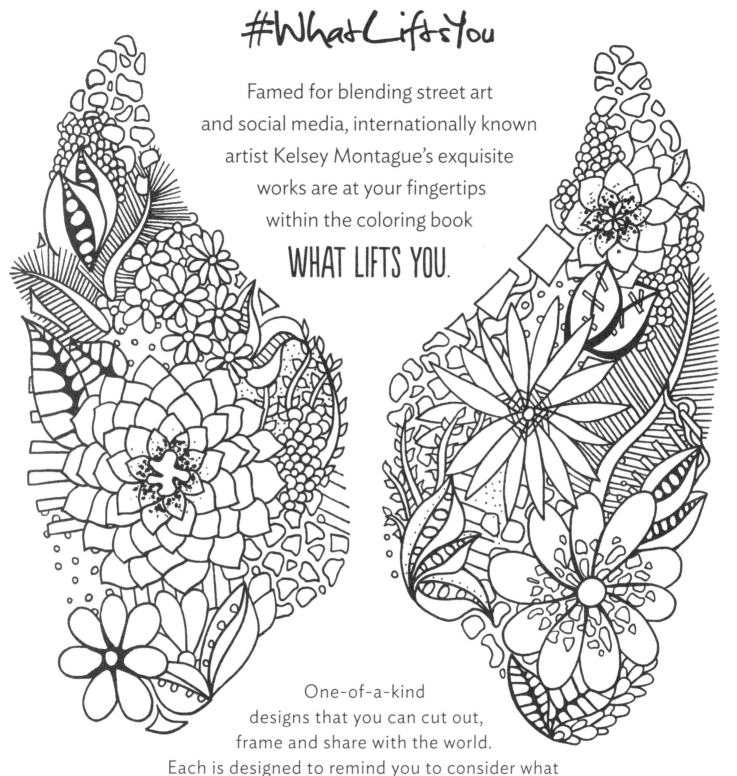
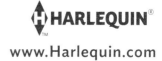